If I am murdered by nobles,
and if they shed my blood, their hands
will remain soiled with my blood.

each other and hate each other, and
for twenty-five years there will
be no nobles in the country....

Excerpt from letter written
by Grigory Rasputin

This book is for Allan and Leonore.

Photographs © 2008: age fotostock/A. H. C.: 51 bottom; AP Images/Museum of Fine Arts, Houston: 50 bottom; Bridgeman Art Library International Ltd., London/New York/Richard and Kailas Icons, London, UK/Private Collection: 28; Corbis Images: 50 top, 65 (Bettmann), 57 (Robert L. Bracklow/Photo Collection Alexander Alland, Sr.), 53 top (Hulton-Deutsch Collection), 26 (William Henry Jackson), 18 (Keystone), 82; Getty Images: 93 (Hulton Archive), 48 top (Roger-Viollet); Hoover Institution Archives, Stanford University/Russian Pictorial Collection: 51 top, 79; Leon Dotan/Private Collection: 49 top; Library of Congress, Prints and Photographs Division/Sergei Mikhailovich Prokudin-Gorskii Collection: 35, 44, 47, 48 bottom; Sovfoto/Eastfoto: 53 bottom, 96, 103 (TASS), 10, 111; The Art Archive/Picture Desk/Dagli Orti/ Domenica del Corriere: 67; The Image Works: 49 bottom, 85 (Ann Ronan Picture Library/HIP), 98 (Mary Evans Picture Library), 52, 91 (C. Walker/Topham); University of Texas Libraries, University of Texas at Austin, Perry-Casteneda Library, Map Collection: 61.

Illustrations by XNR Productions, Inc.: 4, 5, 8, 9
Cover art, page 8 inset by Mark Summers
Chapter art by Roland Sarkany

Library of Congress Cataloging-in-Publication Data

Goldberg, Enid A.
Grigory Rasputin : holy man or mad monk? / by Enid A. Goldberg and Norman Itzkowitz.
p. cm. — (A wicked history)
Includes bibliographical references and index.
ISBN-13: 978-0-531-12594-6 (lib. bdg.) 978-0-531-13896-0 (pbk.)
ISBN-10: 0-531-12594-7 (lib. bdg.) 0-531-13896-8 (pbk.)
1. Rasputin, Grigori Efimovich, ca. 1870-1916—Juvenile literature. 2.
Russia—Court and courtiers—Biography—Juvenile literature. 3.
Russia—History—Nicholas II, 1894-1917—Juvenile literature. I.
Itzkowitz, Norman. II. Title.
DK254.R3G65 2007
947.08'3092—dc22
[B]

2007001692

Tod Olson, Series Editor
Marie O'Neill, Art Director
Allicette Torres, Cover Design
SimonSays Design!, Book Design and Production

© 2008 Scholastic Inc.

Grigory Rasputin

Holy Man
or
Mad Monk?

ENID A. GOLDBERG &
NORMAN ITZKOWITZ

Franklin Watts
An Imprint of Scholastic Inc.
New York   Toronto   London   Auckland   Sydney
Mexico City   New Delhi   Hong Kong
Danbury, Connecticut

Rasputin's Russia, 1900

Rasputin was born a poor peasant in Siberia. He made himself known—for better or worse—all across Russia.

KEY

A Rasputin's birthplace, 1869

B Monastery where Rasputin studied to become a holy man

C City where Rasputin first met important leaders in the Orthodox church

D Russia's capital city. Rasputin arrived in 1903, looking for a way to meet the tsar

E Naval base where Japanese warships sunk the Russian fleet in 1905

F Village where the tsar and his family were executed by revolutionaries, 1918

Map shows boundaries of 1900.
Map is a Lambert Azimuthal equal-area
projection, not a Mercator projection.

miles
0   500   1,000

0   500   1,000
kilometers

Siberia

RUSSIA

Trans-Siberian Railroad

Lake
Baikal

Sea of
Okhotsk

Pacific
Ocean

Vladivostok

N

Port Arthur **E**

CHINA

TABLE OF CONTENTS

PART I: THE YOUNG RASPUTIN

PART 2: LOOKING FOR GOD

PART 3: IN THE CITY OF THE TSARS

A Wicked Web

A look at the allies and enemies of Grigory Rasputin.

Family and Friends

EFIM RASPUTIN ▬▬▬ ANNA RASPUTIN
his father — his mother

PRASKOVYA RASPUTIN
Grigory Rasputin's wife

MARIA, VARVARA, AND DIMITRI
their daughters and son

GEORGE SASONOV
a newspaper man;
also a friend of Rasputin

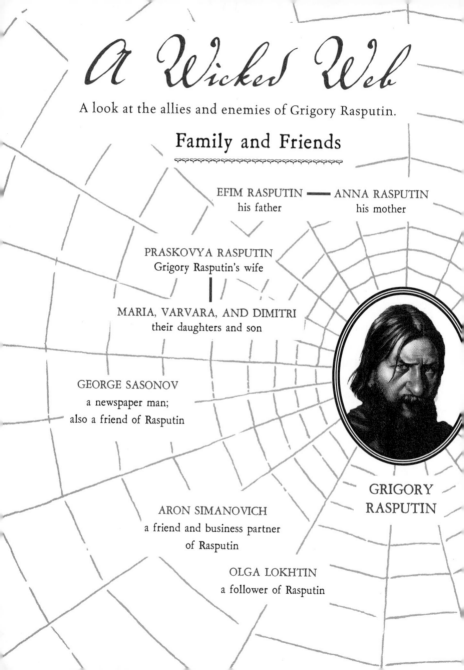

ARON SIMANOVICH
a friend and business partner
of Rasputin

OLGA LOKHTIN
a follower of Rasputin

GRIGORY
RASPUTIN

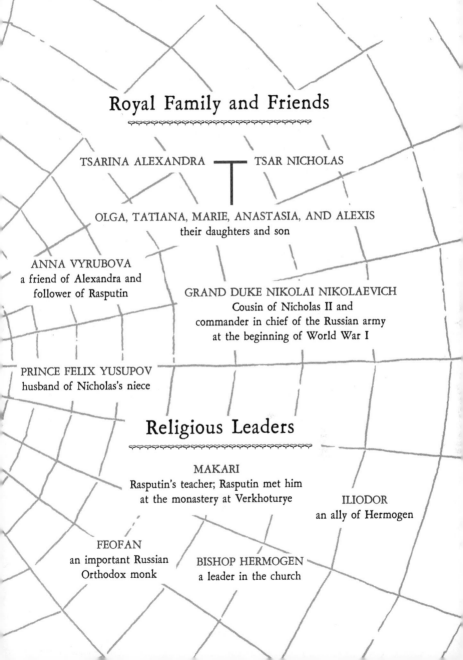

Royal Family and Friends

TSARINA ALEXANDRA ——— TSAR NICHOLAS

OLGA, TATIANA, MARIE, ANASTASIA, AND ALEXIS
their daughters and son

ANNA VYRUBOVA
a friend of Alexandra and
follower of Rasputin

GRAND DUKE NIKOLAI NIKOLAEVICH
Cousin of Nicholas II and
commander in chief of the Russian army
at the beginning of World War I

PRINCE FELIX YUSUPOV
husband of Nicholas's niece

Religious Leaders

MAKARI
Rasputin's teacher; Rasputin met him
at the monastery at Verkhoturye

ILIODOR
an ally of Hermogen

FEOFAN
an important Russian
Orthodox monk

BISHOP HERMOGEN
a leader in the church

GRIGORY RASPUTIN, 1869–1916

THE NIGHT WAS COLD. A hush had fallen over the city. Piles of snow stood high around the apartment building of Grigory Rasputin, trusted adviser to the Empress of Russia. At 11 P.M. a fancy gray car pulled up to the building. Rasputin had been invited to a midnight tea by the wealthy Prince Yusupov. His ride had arrived.

Friends had warned Rasputin not to go out. His enemies were plotting against him, they said. Any day now, he could be murdered. But Rasputin refused to listen. After all, he was the most powerful man in the land. He was God's messenger to the rulers of Russia. At least that was what he told his followers.

Besides, Yusupov was married to the beautiful Princess Irina. Rasputin had a weakness for beautiful women. He was excited to meet the princess.

As usual, Rasputin arranged his long brown hair to cover an ugly bump on his forehead. He combed his beard neatly. "Do not fear," he told his daughter. "Nothing can happen to me unless it is God's will." Rasputin climbed into the car with the prince and drove off.

The car pulled up to Yusupov's palace. The prince led Rasputin to the cellar. A warm fire burned in one corner. On a table, Yusupov had laid out several glasses of wine and a tray of cakes. The sound of music came from upstairs.

But there was no party at the palace. Upstairs, several of Yusupov's friends waited behind a door. One of them had added poison to the cakes and the wine. When the time came, the friends would help carry out Rasputin's dead body.

In the cellar, Yusupov offered his guest two cakes. Rasputin ate. Then he drank the poisoned wine.

Yusupov waited. But Rasputin seemed only to relax. He saw a guitar and asked the prince to play. "Play something cheerful," he said. So the prince played and sang.

After two hours, Rasputin seemed as strong as ever. What was wrong, the prince wondered? Was it true what some people said about this strange man? Was he protected by the forces of evil?

Yusupov excused himself. He went upstairs and got a gun. He came back down and found Rasputin sitting at the table. He told Rasputin to look at a cross and say a prayer. The prince stood over his guest and pointed the gun. He was determined to save Russia once and for all from this wicked man.

Like the rest of Grigory Rasputin's life, it was a strange scene. A prince plans a murder. A holy man can't wait to visit a beautiful woman. Rasputin's friends would do anything for him. His enemies would do anything to get rid of him.

Who was this man? Why did some people love him while others hated him? The truth is almost too strange to believe.

The Young Rasputin

CHAPTER 1

Born in Siberia

A peasant boy's future
LOOKS BLEAK.

GRIGORY RASPUTIN WAS BORN IN SIBERIA, a cold land that fills a huge part of northeastern Russia. The year was probably 1869. No one knows for sure. Rasputin's daughter later claimed that a meteor fell at the moment her father was born.

Life in Rasputin's village was hard. Most people made their living as farmers. They were called *muzhiks*, the Russian word for peasants. They lived in small wooden houses. On dark winter nights, a traveler could freeze to death. Spring brought rivers of mud.

During the summer, flies came in swarms.

The village had little contact with the rest of the world. Supplies came by riverboat or wagon. The nearest doctor lived 70 miles away in the town of Tyumen.

Siberia was filled with criminals. The Russians had built prison camps across the frozen land. Police got rid of prisoners by sending them east. Every two weeks, prison barges passed Rasputin's village on the Tura River.

Other people moved to Siberia to get away from the law. Grigory's father, Efim, was probably one of them. Efim drove a horse and wagon for a living. He carried people and goods from town to town. Rumor had it that he got into trouble in the west. Perhaps he had come to Siberia to escape the police.

There, Efim and his wife, Anna, raised their two boys. To some villagers, Grigory seemed strange. He spent a lot of time staring at the sky. His own mother was afraid he was "not quite right in the head."

Grigory's closest friend was his older brother, Dimitri. Like most Siberian boys, they did not go to school. Instead, they learned to farm. They collected firewood. They played in the woods. Many Siberian boys pretended to be soldiers chasing escaped prisoners.

At night, the brothers slept on sheepskins in a small house. Their bathroom was the backyard. This was their life—until one terrible day when Grigory was eight.

RASPUTIN GREW UP POOR. He came from Pokrovskoye, a small town in Siberia, much like this one.

THE MIDDLE OF NOWHERE

SIBERIA WAS PART OF RUSSIA. BUT IT WAS ALSO A WORLD APART. Its frozen plains lay far away from Moscow and St. Petersburg, the big cities of Russia. The tsars, or kings, ruled from St. Petersburg. No tsar had ever visited Siberia.

The cities in the western part of Russia changed with the rest of Europe. But Siberia stayed the same. By the early 1900s, Moscow and St. Petersburg had electric lights. People talked to each other on telephones. They posed for photographs. They watched moving pictures. Many people had cars. They took trains or steamboats when they traveled far.

In Siberia, people lived much the way their grandparents did. Peasants farmed the land. They traveled only by horse and cart. Until he left home, Rasputin saw only pictures of steamboats and trains.

Turn to the map on pages 4–5 to see where Siberia and other places mentioned in this book are located.

CHAPTER 2

Death!

WHEN GRIGORY WAS EIGHT,
he was scarred for life.

ONE HOT SUMMER'S DAY, Grigory and Dimitri went for a swim in the Tura River. They passed some villagers having lunch by the river. The brothers moved upstream and found a good spot to swim. Grigory was eight at the time.

Dimitri jumped in first. He slipped, and the dark water began to pull him deeper. Grigory raced to his brother and tried to pull him out. Instead, his brother pulled him into the river. Then the current carried them both down the river.

The boys floated past the villagers. A farmer saw them. He rushed to the river and dragged the boys back to land.

The two brothers stumbled home. They were alive but shivering with cold. Grigory was a strong child. He was soon as healthy as ever.

Dimitri was not so lucky. He grew sick with pneumonia. Chills ran through his body. He had trouble breathing. Sharp pains stabbed his chest. But no doctor would travel 70 miles to see him.

Dimitri never got better. He was just ten years old when he died.

Grigory had lost his closest friend. He began acting more strangely than before. One minute he was quiet. The next minute he spoke wildly. Some days he walked in the woods for hours. Other days he never left the house. "I never knew what to expect next," his mother remembered years later.

CHAPTER 3

The Magic Touch

Could Grigory really READ MINDS
and HEAL ANIMALS?

AFTER HIS BROTHER'S DEATH, Grigory kept
to himself. He spent more time with animals than
with boys his age. Villagers probably began to whisper
to each other about the strange boy. Did he think he
could talk to horses? And why did he stare at the sky
all day? Was he crazy? Or did he have special powers?
Was he doing the work of God? Or was he possessed
by the devil?

Years later, people told stories about the young
Grigory. Some of these stories came from his

father, Efim. Some came from Grigory's daughter Maria. They said that the boy had strange talents. He could find lost objects. He could tell when a stranger was about to arrive. He knew when someone would die. He could heal sick animals— even sick people.

According to Efim, his son's talents first appeared one day around lunchtime. The family had just sat down to eat. Efim mentioned that one of his horses had hurt its leg. Grigory got up and went to the barn. He put his hand on the horse's leg. He stood in silence with his face to the ceiling. Finally, he spoke to the animal. "You're all better," he said. According to Efim, the horse was cured.

Villagers began to come to Grigory for help, Grigory's daughter claimed. Farmers with bad backs wanted Grigory to heal them. Women asked him to cure their fevers. Some people said he could even read minds.

When Grigory was 12, he supposedly used his powers to catch a thief. Villagers were gathered at

Grigory's home. Someone had recently stolen a horse from a farmer in town. The men wondered who the thief could be. Grigory stretched out a thin finger and pointed to a rich farmer.

Two of the villagers decided to follow the rich farmer home. They found the missing horse in his barn—just as Grigory had predicted.

Most of these stories were written down years after Rasputin's death. Were they true? Could the young Grigory really heal people and read minds? No one knows.

But Grigory Rasputin definitely had one important talent. He was able to make people believe in him. One day that talent would give him power over many thousands of lives.

CHAPTER 4

Grigory the Saint

In the wild forest, Grigory has a VISION OF GOD.

As A CHILD, GRIGORY FOUND POWER—and comfort—in religion. And he was not alone. Like most Siberian peasants, people in the village believed strongly in God. The tallest building in town was the Russian Orthodox church.

Every Sunday, Grigory gathered with the other villagers for the Orthodox service. As he entered the church, his eyes had to get used to the dark. Rows of candles gave off the only light. Smoke rose from

CHURCHES LIKE THIS ONE were the center of Russian life in the late 1800s. Grigory said he first saw God when he was 14.

burning incense. The air smelled rich and sweet.

Paintings called icons hung from the walls. The icons showed holy figures like Mary, the mother of Jesus. These images looked down on the worshippers with long faces and large eyes.

One painting showed the thin face of Saint Simeon. Simeon had grown up along the Tura River.

Sick peasants from miles away visited his grave. They rubbed their bodies with dirt from around the coffin. People said that Simeon's dirt had healed thousands of peasants.

In church, Grigory and the other villagers left their hard lives behind for a couple of hours. They thought about the holy lives of saints like Simeon. They listened to the priest chant verses from the Bible. They joined in, chanting in slow, dreamy voices.

When Grigory was 14, one service had a special effect on him. The priest read from the Bible. Grigory listened carefully. "Behold, the Kingdom of God is within you," the priest cried. The words hit Grigory like a ray of light.

When the service ended, Grigory walked to the forest. He lay under a tall tree with thin, green needles. Suddenly he felt a "golden glow." Then the warmth burst into "a blinding white flash."

The priest had said that everyone carries God inside him. Now Grigory understood what the priest had meant. He felt that he could almost see God right there in front of him.

This strange experience in the woods was Grigory's first religious vision. After that day, he said, he loved to walk in the woods, "dreaming of God."

Many villagers, however, remembered a different side of Grigory. They remembered him as a drunk and a thief.

RELIGIOUS ICONS had a powerful effect on Grigory. This Russian icon shows baby Jesus and his mother, Mary.

CHAPTER 5

Grigory the Sinner

GRIGORY STEALS, DRINKS,
and chases girls.

As A TEENAGER, Grigory may have felt God within him. But he still got into plenty of trouble. He started drinking vodka at 15, said one villager. When he got drunk, he liked to race his father's horses around the yard. Sometimes, he got caught with girls. More than once, he was beaten by a girl's angry father.

When Efim needed help, Grigory drove the family cart to Tyumen. He often came back drunk. On one trip, he lost a load of furs. Grigory claimed the furs had been stolen by robbers. The villagers thought he had sold the furs and spent the money on vodka.

At least once, Grigory was caught in the act. A farmer found him stealing fence poles. The farmer tried to take Grigory to the police. Grigory swung an ax at the man. But the farmer was tough. He said he hit Grigory "so hard that blood ran out of his nose and his mouth."

Later in life, Grigory tried to explain his bad behavior. He was never happy as a teenager, he said. He did not like to work, and farming was hard labor. Night after night he lay awake. "I was unsatisfied," he said. "I couldn't find an answer to many things. I was sad, and I took to drinking."

At 19, it looked as though Grigory might settle down. He met a young woman named Praskovya at a dance. She was pretty and hard working. Like Grigory, she loved to sing and dance. Six months after they met, the couple got married.

Grigory and his new bride moved in with Grigory's parents. Yet Grigory's troubles continued to pile up. Not long after the fence post theft, he stole again. Grigory and two friends took several horses. The two friends were kicked out of the village. Grigory was allowed to stay. But police were still investigating the furs and the fence poles. Grigory was in real danger.

Grigory talked it over with his wife. They decided he needed to leave for a while. About 250 miles to the northeast lay the Verkhoturye monastery. A monastery is a place where men go to devote their lives to God. The monks there lived simple lives. They prayed and studied the Bible. They kept watch over the bones of Saint Simeon, which were stored there.

No one knows exactly why Grigory wanted to visit the monastery. Grigory later said he was ready to give up his evil ways. He wanted to learn to live a holy life. The villagers didn't believe it for a second. Rasputin simply needed to escape the law, they said.

Either way, Grigory decided to leave. He packed a few things in a bag. He set out on foot for the monastery. It was the beginning of the rest of his life.

PART 2

Looking
for
God

A Wise Man

GRIGORY FINDS
a teacher in the forest.

AFTER A COUPLE OF WEEKS on the road, Grigory reached the Ural Mountains. There, he saw a group of white buildings topped with domes. This was the monastery at Verkhoturye.

The monks took Grigory in as a student. They gave him a room with a cold stone floor. For three months, he slept on a wooden bed with a thin mat. He did farm work to pay for his room and food. He ate meals with the monks. They talked about the Bible. But Grigory's real education came from outside the monastery walls.

AS A YOUNG MAN, Grigory went to this
monastery in Verkhoturye. Did he want to lead a holy life?
Or was he just escaping the law?

The monks told Grigory about a famous holy man named Makari. Makari and other holy men lived in the forest outside the monastery. They were known as "elders." Ordinary Russians often traveled hundreds of miles to visit an elder. The elders gave advice about religion.

Most elders chose to be very poor. Many ate only black bread and water. They tried to wipe their lives clean of sin, or evil behavior. Some wandered for years. They went on pilgrimages to visit holy places. They begged for their food. When they settled down, they lived simply. At Verkhoturye, they slept in huts with dirt floors. Some lived in caves and rarely saw other people. They spent their days praying and thinking about God.

Grigory visited Makari every day. He learned that Makari had once been a wealthy man. But the elder wasted his money on drinking, women, and gambling. Then he forced himself to pay for his sins. He gave up all pleasures. As penance, or payment, Makari wore chains on his legs. He fasted, going without food for days.

Grigory told Makari his own life story. He talked about his crimes. He spoke of his desire for women. He also told Makari about his vision in the forest.

Makari told Grigory that his vision of God was real. It was a sign that Grigory had a special purpose in life. He must become a man of God. He should help others to see the truth. "God has chosen you for a great achievement," Makari told him.

What would that achievement be?

C H A P T E R   7

On the Road

Grigory goes in
SEARCH OF GOD.

AFTER THREE MONTHS, Rasputin returned to his village. His neighbors saw right away that he had changed. He had stopped drinking and smoking. He wouldn't eat meat. He began to learn to read. God made me see the truth, he explained. "I gave up drinking. I followed another path."

That path led in a strange direction. Villagers often saw Rasputin talking to himself. He mumbled lines from the Bible while he walked. In church, he stood up in the middle of the service. He waved his arms. He sang loudly and out of tune. "He seems to have become a madman," said one neighbor. Some people thought the beating from the farmer had damaged his brain.

Rasputin said the visions came more often now. He said he saw Jesus walking along the Tura River. One night, he slept under an icon of Mary, the mother of Jesus. When he woke up, he said later, he saw the icon crying.

He claimed the painting spoke to him. "I am weeping for the sins of mankind," it said. "Go, wander, and [cleanse] the people of their sins."

Rasputin took the icon's advice. He put on a sheepskin coat. Then he carefully packed a backpack. He took a Bible, a cross, and a knife. He packed a loaf of bread and a bottle for water. He took one extra shirt and a pair of sandals. Then he said goodbye to his wife. Like Makari and other elders, Rasputin became a wanderer.

Most of the time, Rasputin traveled by foot.

He walked as much as 30 miles a day. He visited monasteries and other holy places. On his first trip, he traveled 2,000 miles to a famous monastery in Greece.

Peasants respected the wanderers. They admired Rasputin's faith in God. Often, they let him sleep in a barn or cellar. They fed him. In return, Rasputin promised to light candles for them in holy places.

Every day, Rasputin looked more and more like an elder. His beard grew long. His teeth were brown. He fasted for days at a time. He went months without bathing or changing his clothes. As he walked, he mumbled a prayer to himself. "Lord Jesus Christ, Son of God, have mercy on me, a sinner."

Slowly, people across Siberia began to learn Rasputin's name. He stayed with a group of fisherman for a while. He taught them verses from the Bible. He told people he had been sent to them by God.

In the fall, Rasputin would return home from his wanderings. Sometimes he had picked up followers on the road. Usually, they were women.

Still, his wife, Praskovya, was happy to see him. She had been taking care of the farm all summer. Between 1897 and 1900, they had three children, Dimitri, Maria, and Varvara.

Rasputin settled in for the winters. He told stories of his travels. He talked about tall churches where he could feel God's presence. He talked about the hardships he suffered. There were wolf attacks and terrible storms. Sometimes, robbers came after him. "I would say to them, it is not mine but God's," he said. "Take from me. I give it to you gladly."

But Rasputin experienced more than hunger and danger on his travels. There were other stories as well—stories that he wasn't as eager to tell.

CHAPTER 8

Secret Worship

What was Rasputin doing
IN THAT CAVE?

Back IN THE VILLAGE, Rasputin acted like an elder. Most people laughed. How could that drunken thief turn into a holy man? He was a fake, they said.

But Rasputin had a different effect on some people—particularly women. His eyes glowed as he told stories of faraway places. He stared straight at his listeners. They, too, could find God inside them, he said.

A small group of followers began to gather around Rasputin. They wanted his advice about God. They brought sick children to him. They asked him to use his healing powers.

Rasputin gave his new followers a place to worship. He dug a cave under his barn. He hung icons on the earth walls. He lit candles in the dark.

No one really knew what went on during these meetings. But the villagers spread rumors. They said that women washed Rasputin and drank the bathwater. Rasputin sang and chanted. They all danced and ran around a fire. Finally, they fell on the floor together.

Rumors from Rasputin's travels reached the village, too. In 1900, a woman complained that Rasputin tried to kill her. She said she had seen Rasputin attacking two young women in a field. When she tried to protect them, Rasputin attacked her. Police looked into the woman's charge. They decided she was lying.

And there were other enemies. The village priest complained about him to Russian Orthodox leaders. Rasputin was part of a cult, the priest said.

This was a very serious charge. At the time, there

were many cults in Russia. All across the country, people met secretly to worship in strange ways. They gathered in dark cellars and barns. They met in forest clearings.

But most of these cults were against the law. If a cult member was caught, he or she could be whipped. He could be sent to jail for years.

It was true that Rasputin had come across several secret cults during his travels. And several of them may have influenced him—particularly one group called the *khlysty*.

The *khlysty* believed in sinning as a way to get closer to God. According to the *khlysty*, after a person sinned, he could ask God for forgiveness. God would forgive him, and the person would then feel closer to God than ever.

Later in his life, Rasputin used this idea to seduce women. He'd tell them that he was a "higher being." "One can be saved only through me," he'd say. "To achieve this, one ought to merge with me, body and soul."

Still, no one ever proved that Rasputin was a member of the *khlysty*. After the village priests complained about Rasputin, the church investigation found him innocent. Police questioned his followers about the meetings in the cave. They said they simply prayed and fasted.

Rasputin managed to stay out of trouble—as he would again and again. Still, by 1903, Rasputin was outgrowing his tiny village. He wanted a bigger audience. He had great things to do, Makari had said. It was time to prove the elder right.

MAKARI, THE ELDER, lived simply in a hut near Verkhoturye. He said Rasputin had a special purpose in life.

CHAPTER 9

The Big City

Rasputin conquers the priests—
AND THE WOMEN—of Kazan.

IN 1903, RASPUTIN arrived in Kazan. This was a key city for the Orthodox Church. It was home to one of Russia's four religious universities. Many church leaders lived there. Rasputin was ready to meet them.

First, Rasputin met the rich businessmen of the city. He also met their wives. According to one story, Rasputin was brought to Kazan by a woman named Madame Bashmakova.

Madame Bashmakova's husband had recently died. She and her friends were wealthy and bored. Many of them were depressed. They went to Rasputin for spiritual advice—and he thrilled them.

He showed up in their expensive homes with his stringy hair and dirty fingernails. He ate with his hands. He was proud of the fact that he was a simple peasant. The women loved him for his honesty. Here was a real Siberian holy man, they thought.

Rasputin held a strange power over the people he met. He told tales of his wanderings. He spoke of his visions. He seemed to know people's secrets. He might tell one woman she was unhappy. He would tell another she was ill.

As Rasputin talked, he stared at his listeners. And they always remembered his eyes. They "seemed to pierce you," said one of the Kazan women. She insisted he had "the gift of hypnotizing those around him."

Before long, rumors again began to fly. What was this strange peasant doing with the women of Kazan? One woman said a "respectable lady" had shared a bed with Rasputin. Another woman saw Rasputin coming out of a bathhouse with two young women.

Rasputin soon met the bishop of Kazan. Had the rumors reached the bishop? No one knows. If they had, the bishop didn't believe them. Or he simply didn't care.

The bishop told Rasputin to go to St. Petersburg. Rasputin must have liked the idea. St. Petersburg was the capital of the country. It was the home of Tsar Nicholas and his wife, Alexandra. Rasputin would be close to the most powerful people in Russia. It would be a great achievement for a simple peasant.

Rasputin went home with a letter from the bishop. The letter introduced Rasputin to an important bishop in St. Petersburg. Here, it said, was a "man of God."

THE CITY OF KAZAN was home to many important church leaders. Rasputin won them over when he visited there in 1903.

Rasputin in Pictures

FROM THE COUNTRY

Rasputin came from a small village in Siberia called Pokrovskoye. When he returned from his travels, he liked to spend time with his children (from left to right), Maria, Varvara, and Dimitri.

SAINT OR SINNER?

As a young man, Rasputin was religious. But he was also a troublemaker. Once, he had to get out of town—and quick. He decided to go here, to the monastery at Verkhoturye.

POWERFUL FRIENDS

In 1903, Rasputin arrived in St. Petersburg. There he met two important religious leaders, Bishop Hermogen (center), and the preacher Iliodor (right).

A LADIES' MAN

The wealthy families of St. Petersburg welcomed Rasputin into their homes. He told women there that he could help them get closer to God. All they had to do was follow his instructions.

FRIEND OF THE ROYALS

Tsar Nicholas II and Tsarina
Alexandra first met Rasputin in
1905. Rasputin quickly made friends
with their five children (from left to
right), Olga, Marie, Anastasia, Alexis,
and Tatiana.

THE ROMANOV DYNASTY

The Romanov dynasty had ruled Russia for
300 years. The family had wealth and power.
And Nicholas and Alexandra wanted to
preserve it all for their son Alexis. This jewel
was part of the Romanov collection.

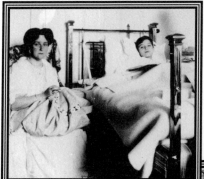

A FRAGILE HEIR

Nicholas and Alexandra's son Alexis was heir to the throne. His parents came to believe that only Rasputin could keep him alive.

THE WORLD AT WAR

In 1914, World War I began. Despite his son's illness, the tsar took Alexis to the front with him. While the tsar was gone, Rasputin's power grew. He and Alexandra took over the business of running the country.

PUBLIC OPINION

Russian newspapers criticized the influence Rasputin had over
the tsar and tsarina. In this cartoon, the tsar and tsarina appear as
puppets under Rasputin's control.

BEAUTIFUL SCHEMERS

By 1916, many members of the nobility felt they had to do something about Rasputin. Prince Felix Yusupov plotted to kill him. He lured Rasputin to his house by promising he would meet Irina.

ICED

Rasputin's mangled body was pulled from a frozen river in December 1916.

PART 3

In the City
of the Tsars

A City in Conflict

Rasputin arrives in St. Petersburg, A CITY ON THE EDGE.

NEAR THE END OF 1903, Rasputin boarded a steamboat. He went up the Tura River to Tyumen. There, he paid 15 rubles—about $7.50—for a train ticket. He got on the new Trans-Siberian railway. The train rattled 1,000 miles across Russia. Finally, it arrived in St. Petersburg.

Rasputin stepped off the train into a strange new world. St. Petersburg was the center of power in Russia. Gray statues of the tsars towered over the streets. Huge palaces stood on the banks of the Neva River. Gold church domes shone in the sun.

St. Petersburg was beautiful. But when Rasputin arrived, it was on the edge of revolution.

Russia was a monarchy, a country led by a ruler who inherits the throne. A single family—the Romanovs—had ruled the country for 300 years. Nicholas II was the eighteenth tsar in the Romanov family. The tsars made all important decisions in the country.

The tsar's family and a small group of nobles lived

ST. PETERSBURG WAS A JEWEL of a city when Rasputin arrived in 1903. But its beauty was misleading. Revolution was brewing.

in luxury in St. Petersburg. They went boating on the Neva. At night, they went out to the opera or the ballet They went on hunting trips to Poland. They relaxed during beach vacations near the Black Sea.

Meanwhile, Russia was changing fast around them. In St. Petersburg, new factories went up every year. Peasants arrived from villages like Rasputin's to find jobs. They worked 11 hours on weekdays and 10 hours on Saturday. They made less than 50 cents a day. Their wages were barely enough to feed a family. Many workers survived on black bread and cabbage soup. Whole families slept in single rooms.

Russian workers were angry. In 1903, they went on strike, closing down factories. They demanded higher wages and shorter workdays. They called for a more democratic form of government. They wanted to elect their own leaders. They wanted the freedom to speak their minds. Some even wanted complete change, or revolution. They wanted to get rid of the tsar.

Nicholas and Alexandra hated the protesters.

Nicholas was a weak leader and didn't know much about politics. But he and Alexandra did not want to give up power. They felt that God had given the tsars the right to rule Russia.

The royal couple also feared for their lives. Some of the protesters were willing to kill for their beliefs. In 1881, Nicholas's grandfather, Alexander II, had been killed in a bomb attack. And since 1900, revolutionaries had killed three government officials.

Nicholas and Alexandra rarely went out in public. They stayed in a place called the tsar's village, a half-hour from the city. It was surrounded by guards and a tall iron fence.

Rasputin arrived in this divided city in the middle of winter. He said he wanted to build a church in his village. He had come to St. Petersburg to raise money.

Some of his new friends thought he had a different goal. From the start, they said, Rasputin wanted to meet the rulers of Russia. It seemed impossible. To Rasputin, it was a challenge.

CHAPTER 11

Powerful Allies

Rasputin wins over some IMPORTANT PEOPLE.

WHEN RASPUTIN got off the train in St. Petersburg, he was dressed like a beggar. He wore an old gray coat. His pants had holes in them. His shoes were held together with tar. He smelled like he hadn't bathed in months.

None of that seemed to matter. Rasputin quickly made friends in the Church.

First, he brought his letter to a monk named Feofan. Feofan was a professor of religion. He welcomed Rasputin and brought him to a class.

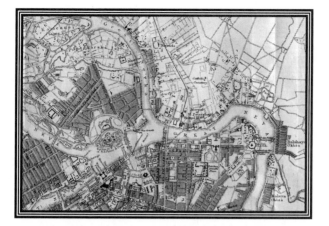

THIS MAP SHOWS ST. PETERSBURG around the time
Rasputin arrived. With nearly two million people, it was
by far the biggest city Rasputin had seen.

The two men stood in front of a room full of students.
They argued about sin. Feofan said that people must pray
and fast to avoid sin. This made Rasputin angry. "[Go
ahead and] sin, if sin lurks in you," he commanded. "Sin,
[and] then you repent and drive evil from you."

Those were dangerous words. Rasputin sounded
like a *khlyst*. But he didn't seem worried. He simply
stared at Feofan. The teacher backed down. He told
his students that Rasputin was right.

Feofan invited Rasputin to stay with him. Then Feofan spread the word that a powerful new holy man had arrived.

In December, Rasputin met with another church leader, Bishop Hermogen. Hermogen was a strong supporter of the tsar. He hated the protesting workers. He hated democracy. He also hated Jews.

Hermogen had a student named Iliodor who shared his views. Iliodor was a popular preacher. He spoke to huge crowds in public places. He blamed Jews for Russia's problems. Iliodor liked to dress a large doll in Jewish robes. His followers carried the doll to a bonfire and burned it.

To Hermogen and Iliodor, peasants were the real Russians. They believed that if the revolution came, the peasants would support the tsar. Rasputin made them feel as though they were right. Here was a true peasant who loved God and the tsar. He would help them fight against change. He was a man who could help them save Russia.

A History of Hatred

IN 1903, IT WAS DANGEROUS TO BE A JEW IN RUSSIA. For decades, Russian Jews had suffered under unfair laws. They could live only in certain areas. They couldn't own farmland. They couldn't do business on Christian holidays.

A few Jewish businessmen had gotten very wealthy. But most Jews lived in poverty in small villages, or *shtetls*. Many were ready to demand equal rights. They joined the workers' groups that were fighting the tsar.

To people like Iliodor, Jews were the cause of Russia's problems. Some wealthy nobles also lashed out at the Jews. They called themselves the Black Hundred.

The Black Hundred had connections to the Russian secret police. The police helped organize gangs to terrorize Jews. Black Hundred gangs rode through the *shtetls* on horseback. They burned homes. They slashed at people on the streets. These riots were called *pogroms*. Between 1903 and 1906, hundreds of Jews were killed. Thousands were injured. Many thousands more were left homeless.

Anger in the Streets

AN HEIR IS BORN, while
enemies close in on the tsar.

IN 1904, RASPUTIN WENT HOME. He had met
important people in St. Petersburg. One friend reported
that women from the city visited him in his village.
They treated him like an elder. He treated them like
girlfriends. "Rasputin shamelessly embraced and kissed
them," the friend said.

While Rasputin flirted in Siberia, the tsar was in
trouble. In January 1904, Russia went to war with Japan.

The war was a disaster. The Japanese trapped several Russian ships at a navy base called Port Arthur.

In August, Russians got a short break from the bad news. Tsarina Alexandra gave birth to a baby boy. Big guns fired 300 times into the air to celebrate. It was great news for the friends of the tsar. Only a male could take over from the tsar when he died. So far, the royal couple had given birth to four girls. Now, the Romanovs had a son to continue their rule.

TSAR NICHOLAS AND TSARINA ALEXANDRA had five children. Alexis, the only boy, became heir to the throne.

Still, the monarchy itself was in danger. The military defeats made Russians angry. They felt the tsar was leading the country to ruin. More and more workers went on strike. In the countryside, peasants burned barns and killed farm animals. On the battlefront, soldiers refused to obey orders. In St. Petersburg, a government official was blown up when a revolutionary threw a bomb into his carriage.

Protesters demanded that the tsar step down. But Nicholas refused to give in. He tried to crack down on the protests. The secret police arrested hundreds of people. Soldiers moved into the capital.

On January 22, 1905, the tension exploded into violence. At dawn, a crowd of peaceful protesters gathered in St. Petersburg. They marched through the streets. They carried icons and Russian flags. They sang religious songs.

A line of soldiers blocked the way to the tsar's palace. The soldiers had been given extra vodka the night before. They warned the marchers to turn back. Then they opened fire. When the shooting was over, at least 150 people lay dead on the street.

Rasputin heard about the violence. He decided it was time to go back to St. Petersburg. God, he said, had work for him there.

RUSSIAN SOLDIERS ATTACKED PROTESTERS in St. Petersburg on January 22, 1905. The massacre became known as "Bloody Sunday."

CHAPTER 13

Revolution!

Nicholas is forced
TO COMPROMISE.

RASPUTIN CAME BACK to St. Petersburg early in 1905. The city was tense. Police and soldiers patrolled the streets. Assassins plotted their next moves. In February, a bomb killed Alexandra's brother-in-law.

News from the war was no better. In January, Port Arthur surrendered to the Japanese. In May, Japanese warships sunk the Russian fleet off the coast of Japan. The Russians lost 25 ships and 5,000 sailors.

Wealthy nobles were worried. The violence frightened them. News from the war depressed them.

At dinner parties, they talked about Russia's troubles.

Soon, they were talking about Rasputin. And what a great distraction he was!

Rasputin moved in with a newspaper owner named George Sasonov. Sasonov took Rasputin to parties all across St. Petersburg. Everyone wanted to meet the new Siberian holy man.

Rasputin was a crude guest. Sometimes he was shocking. When he met women, he often kissed them on the lips. He asked personal questions: Why are you not married? Are you happy? Do you love your husband? At one house, Rasputin found a wall covered with expensive paintings. He told his hostess she should be ashamed of herself. "Just look at how they live while the peasants starve," he said.

Despite his rudeness, Rasputin was welcomed into St. Petersburg society. The nobles liked to feel close to a true peasant. And Rasputin made them feel closer to God. Soon, rich women were buying him fine clothes. Some even made silk shirts for him.

Little by little, Rasputin got closer to the royal family. He became a regular guest at the home of Grand Duke Nikolai Nikolaevich. The grand duke was the cousin of the tsar.

Word spread quickly among St. Petersburg society that Rasputin had special powers. He had predicted the destruction of the Russian fleet, they said. He also predicted a drought. Feofan said Rasputin could even control the weather.

But Rasputin could not control the violence in the streets. In October, railroad workers went on strike. Everyone in the capital stopped working. The whole country basically shut down. Tsar Nicholas ordered more troops into the streets. It seemed that a revolution was about to begin.

On October 30, Nicholas decided to compromise with the protesters. He signed an order called the October Manifesto. It brought some democracy to Russia. It promised freedom of speech and freedom of religion. It also created a *Duma*, or Congress.

The Russian people would elect the *Duma's* members.

Nicholas and Alexandra had been defeated. The tsar wrote in his diary that night. His head felt "heavy," he said. "Help us, O Lord. Save Russia and grant her peace."

Two weeks later, the royal couple visited the grand duke. Rasputin was there at the time. The tsar simply wrote, "We met the man of God, Grigory." His wife may have been more excited. By this time, Rasputin's talent as a healer was well known.

And the royal couple was keeping a tragic secret from the country. Little Alexis, their son, the *tsarevich*, was terribly ill.

CHAPTER 14

Alexandra's Secrets

The tsarina is DESPERATE for help.

WHEN ALEXANDRA FIRST MET RASPUTIN, she was in a miserable state. Her husband had just given away power to his enemies. What would be left of the tsar's power when their son took over the throne?

More important, would Alexis still be alive? Six weeks after the boy was born, he got a scratch on his stomach. It was a tiny cut, but it wouldn't stop bleeding. Doctors gave the royal couple the bad news.

Their son had a disease called hemophilia. His

blood would not stop flowing after an injury. Small scrapes could make him lose pints of blood. Bruises made him bleed under the skin. A leg or an arm could swell to twice its size. It was terribly painful—and it could be fatal. The disease killed most people by the time they were 30.

The news devastated Nicholas and Alexandra. And they decided to deal with it alone. They told almost no one. They did not want people to know that the heir to the throne was so fragile.

Alexandra grew depressed. She rarely left the palace. She devoted her life to two goals. She pushed her husband to keep the monarchy strong. And she tried desperately to keep Alexis alive.

It was a huge mission, and Alexandra didn't have much help. She was born in Germany and had never learned much Russian. She was shy. She had very few friends. Instead, she relied on a deep faith in God, and in the power of miracles. Four months before she got pregnant with Alexis, she bathed in the waters of a holy well. She was convinced that the bath had produced her son. Could another miracle make Alexis healthy?

By 1906, Rasputin had a reputation as a healer. The grand duke thought Rasputin had cured his sick dog. A rich hostess named Olga Lokhtina swore that Rasputin had cured her of depression and a stomach problem.

That fall, Rasputin was invited to the tsar's palace for the first time. He brought an icon of Simeon, his favorite saint. He embraced Nicholas and Alexandra. He called them "Mama" and "Papa."

He tried to calm their fears about the future. They would survive the protests, he said. The peasants loved them the way children love parents. The revolution would end. The Russian people would support the tsar.

Then, Rasputin was introduced to two-year-old Alexis. He blessed the sick child with the icon. Nicholas and Alexandra were filled with hope. Here was a man who could speak to God. He told them that peace would come. Could he also heal their son?

THE ROYAL DISEASE

HEMOPHILIA IS A RARE DISEASE. Only one in 4,000 people have it—and Alexis was unlucky enough to be one of them.

But he wasn't the only royal heir who could bleed to death at any moment. Between them, the rulers of Russia, Spain, and Germany had five children with hemophilia. How did such a rare disease affect so many princes? They owe it all to Alexis's great grandmother, Queen Victoria of England.

Hemophilia is hereditary. That means that it's passed on from parents to their kids. Women can carry the disease and pass it on. But only males can actually have the disease.

Queen Victoria was a carrier of hemophilia. So were four of her granddaughters—including Alexandra. They married into other royal families to form alliances between countries. And before long, hemophilia was known as "the royal disease."

PART 4

The Rise of Rasputin

CHAPTER 15

The Faith Healer

RASPUTIN WINS the royal couple's trust.

RASPUTIN SETTLED INTO HIS OLD PATTERN. He went home to his village for the winter. In the spring, he returned to St. Petersburg and his new friends. The nobles gave him money to live on.

In 1907, Rasputin visited the palace a few more times. He told the royal couple tales of his wanderings. He played with the children. He prayed with the family. Little by little, Nicholas and Alexandra began to rely on him. Rasputin gave them hope that God was on their side.

That fall, they watched him perform the miracle they had been waiting for.

Rasputin arrived to visit one afternoon. Alexis was bleeding and in pain. The elder went to the boy's bedroom. He said a prayer. Before long, color returned to the boy's face. The bleeding stopped.

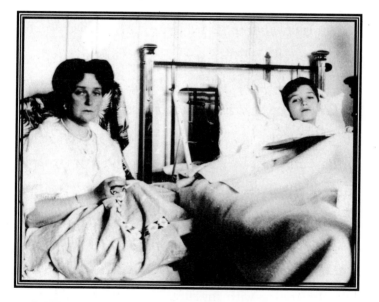

WHEN ALEXIS WAS SICK IN BED, Alexandra (left) often kept watch over him. Only the doctors and Rasputin were told about Alexis's illness.

Nicholas and Alexandra were amazed.

"Be calm. Your son will live," Rasputin told the royal couple. "When he is twenty, his illness will disappear."

After that day, Rasputin became a regular guest at the palace. He played with Alexis and made him laugh. Sometimes he treated the boy with peasant cures. Once he made a paste of oak bark and water. He put it on a cut to stop the bleeding. Often Rasputin simply prayed with the sick boy. Doctors today think he made Alexis calm. The calming effect may have made the boy's blood flow more slowly and stopped the bleeding.

Rasputin also seemed to calm the royal couple. Alexandra suffered from nervousness and headaches. Nicholas drank too much. They looked forward to Rasputin's visits. Nicholas told a guard at the palace that he liked to talk to Rasputin when he felt troubled. "I feel at peace with myself afterward," he said.

Nicholas and Alexandra thought that Rasputin brought them protection from God. According to a friend of the royal family, "They believed in the strength of his prayers." They began to call Rasputin "Our Friend."

By the summer of 1908, Rasputin was getting bold. He bragged about his influence on Nicholas and Alexandra. He played "a special role with the tsar," he said. He was going to "save Russia."

But some people were already getting ready to save Russia from Rasputin. The secret police had begun to gather information about him. Palace guards took notes on his visits to Nicholas and Alexandra. Agents collected stories about his relationships with women. Russia's prime minister, Peter Stolypin, kept the information in a file. Stolypin hated Rasputin. He wanted him sent back to Siberia. And he wasn't the only one.

THE SECRET POLICE

THEY WERE WATCHING EVERYONE. For decades, revolutionaries had been trying to change Russia. And for decades, secret police had been spying on them.

This secret organization was called the Okhrana. It was started by Alexander II four years before he was killed.

The Okhrana's main job was to protect the royal family. Okhrana spies went to workers' meetings. They read the mail of suspected revolutionaries. They paid workers to tell them about secret plans.

Okhrana agents arrested anyone who criticized the tsar. Some suspects were killed without a trial. Thousands more were exiled.

As Rasputin got to know the tsar, the Okhrana became curious. They watched him around the clock. At one point, five agents watched him full-time.

CHAPTER 16

Rumors, Rumors

RASPUTIN IS BEHAVING BADLY,
but the royal couple doesn't care.

INSIDE THE PALACE, Rasputin won friends. He met Alexandra's closest friend, a woman named Anna Vyrubova. She lived in the tsar's village. Anna adored Rasputin. He spent many days at her home.

Outside the palace, Rasputin won followers. He appeared with the preacher Iliodor in public. The two holy men preached to huge crowds.

In private, Rasputin got his own apartment and met more and more women. Visitors came often to ask for advice. They ate black bread and drank tea.

WOMEN WERE DRAWN TO RASPUTIN'S magnetic
personality. They often gathered for parties in the
holy man's St. Petersburg apartment.

Some of them saved the bread crusts to display in
their homes. Women clipped Rasputin's fingernails.
They kept the nails as treasures. Some of them sewed
the fingernails onto their dresses.

But as Rasputin became famous, he began to make
enemies. One of them was his old friend Feofan. In the
summer of 1909, Feofan visited Siberia with Rasputin. He
was shocked at the way Rasputin acted. Rasputin didn't

fast when he was supposed to. He left church services early. And Feofan had begun to hear stories. Rasputin took women to bathhouses. Perhaps he even seduced them.

At the beginning of 1910, these stories reached the palace. Feofan complained to the royal couple. At the same time, a newspaper published a series of articles about Rasputin. The paper printed a letter from a woman who said that Rasputin had seduced her. It also suggested that Rasputin was a member of the *khlyst* cult.

Then, little Alexis's nurse went to Alexandra with a shocking tale. Rasputin had attacked her, she said. The children's governess also talked to the tsar. She told Nicholas that she thought Rasputin shouldn't go near his daughters.

Prime Minister Stolypin added to the complaints. He told the tsar that Rasputin was a danger to the monarchy. The rumors about him were embarrassing. They made people lose faith in the tsar.

But nothing could make Nicholas and Alexandra lose faith in Rasputin. One by one, they got rid of

Rasputin's enemies. Feofan was given a job in Crimea, hundreds of miles from the capital. The nurse was accused of lying and was eventually fired. Privately, the tsar decided to get rid of Stolypin. Then he told the governess that he could not get along without Rasputin. "I have lived all these years only thanks to his prayers," he said.

Rasputin was safe, for now. But he decided he should leave the capital for a while. In the spring of 1911, he went on a pilgrimage to Palestine. Hopefully, things would calm down while he was gone.

CHAPTER 17

"Miserable Worms"

Rasputin's enemies GAIN STRENGTH.

RASPUTIN RETURNED in the summer of 1911. He was as powerful as ever. The tsar was ready to replace Stolypin, the prime minister. He asked Rasputin to help him make the decision. The tsar also needed to choose a new leader of the Russian Orthodox Church. He made sure that Rasputin met the man first.

Rasputin felt as though his enemies couldn't touch him. He went to visit Iliodor. The two men preached together in public. "Yes, my enemies have attacked me," Rasputin said. "They think my end has come. It makes you laugh! It's their end that's here. Not mine. Who are they? Worms crawling in a pot of cabbage. Miserable worms and nothing more."

But the "worms" were gathering strength. And even Iliodor was about to join them. Iliodor had traveled to Siberia with Rasputin in 1910. He heard the rumors about Rasputin's behavior with women. He also listened to Rasputin's boasts. "The tsar cannot breathe without me," Rasputin told him.

Then, Rasputin made a mistake. He showed Iliodor a pile of letters from Alexandra. The tsarina wrote Rasputin long, affectionate letters. She was extremely grateful to Rasputin for keeping her son alive. And the way she expressed her gratitude could—to an outsider—sound as though she were in love with Rasputin.

Like the rest of Russia, Iliodor knew nothing about Alexis's illness. Iliodor misunderstood the letters—and he was disgusted. He also knew that the letters could be useful to him. He stole a couple of them.

At the end of 1911, Iliodor and Bishop Hermogen decided that Rasputin had to be stopped. They called him to a meeting at a monastery. They cornered Rasputin in a dark room with stone walls. The bishop held a large wooden cross. Rasputin was trapped.

One by one, the men listed Rasputin's crimes. Rasputin had lied to the tsar and tsarina, they said. He had taken women to bathhouses.

Finally, the Bishop demanded, "Is it true?"

"It's true," Rasputin said meekly. "It's all true."

Hermogen went crazy with anger. He hit Rasputin with the cross. Rasputin fell to his knees. He swore never to touch a woman again. He would leave St. Petersburg, he said. He would never see the royal family again.

Rasputin convinced the men to let him go. Then he went home and sent a message to the royal family. Hermogen and Iliodor had tried to murder him, he said.

Within a month, Hermogen and Iliodor were gone. The tsar banned them from St. Petersburg.

But for Rasputin, the trouble wasn't over yet.

CHAPTER 18

Another Miracle

RASPUTIN GETS HIMSELF
out of trouble again.

EARLY IN 1912, all of St. Petersburg was talking about Rasputin. Newspapers were full of stories about him. Reporters told about the beating in the monastery. They accused Rasputin of being a *khlyst*.

Then Iliodor struck again. In February, he sent one of Alexandra's letters to a newspaper. The next morning, Russians were shocked at what they read. Alexandra called Rasputin "my beloved." She spoke of kissing his hands and resting her head on his shoulder. "My heart is longing," she said. "I am waiting for you."

The tsar was furious. He knew his wife was not in love with Rasputin. And yet, the newspapers made it sound as though she were. The tsar made it illegal for newspapers to print Rasputin's name. But Rasputin's name sold papers. Many publishers printed the stories and gladly paid the fines.

A NEWSPAPER CARTOON ASKS:
Who is really ruling Russia?

Rasputin's enemies were everywhere. One by one, they came to the tsar to complain. A member of the *Duma* spoke out in public. He wondered if the tsar was really in control of the country. "You must ask—who is playing master at the top?" he said.

Rasputin knew it was time to go home again. He left for Siberia. Alexandra was sad to see her trusted friend go. She depended on him. So did her son. But

Rasputin had become a danger to the tsar.

It looked like Rasputin might be finished. But he wasn't out of miracles yet.

In the summer of 1912, the royal family went on vacation. They stayed at a hunting lodge in Poland. In August, Alexis stumbled. He hit his thigh as he was getting into a rowboat. But he seemed to recover after a few days.

Then in October, Alexis started having terrible pain. For 11 days, he lay in bed at the hunting lodge. His face grew pale. Sometimes he cried out in pain. "Mama, help me," he kept saying. "Won't you help me?"

Alexandra tried. She prayed. She sat beside him. She stayed awake all night. Nicholas couldn't stand to see his son in pain. At one point, he left the room in tears.

The family expected Alexis to die. But Alexandra had one last hope. She sent a telegram to Rasputin and asked him to pray. Rasputin sent a message back.

"God has seen your tears," it said. "Do not grieve. The Little One will not die."

The next day, Alexis felt better. In a few days, he recovered. Once again, here was proof. And this time, Nicholas was convinced: God answered Rasputin's prayers. How could the family get along without him?

A SAILOR KEPT WATCH OVER ALEXIS at all times. He carried the sick boy everywhere.

CHAPTER 19

A Surprise Attack

RASPUTIN IS KNIFED;
the world goes to war.

IN 1913, RASPUTIN WAS BACK in St. Petersburg. It was a big year for Russia. The tsar's family, the Romanovs, had ruled the country for 300 years. All of Russia celebrated. And the tsar gave Rasputin a special place at the celebrations.

Rasputin's enemies couldn't believe it. All the secrets had come out last year. How could the tsar still support this man?

But Nicholas did support him. Rasputin knew it. And he began to act as though he couldn't be harmed.

Rasputin had a favorite restaurant in St. Petersburg. It was called the Villa Rhode. The owners gave him a private room whenever he called. Visitors came to eat and drink with him. There was good food and plenty of wine. There were singers and musicians. Rasputin began to drink heavily again. He danced. He handed out pieces of paper with words of wisdom on them. "Go not from the way of love, for love is your mother," one of them said.

But most people weren't there for wisdom. They were there to ask for favors. Women wanted to get their husbands out of jail. Businessmen wanted special privileges from the tsar. Politicians wanted important jobs in the government. They knew that the tsar listened to Rasputin. Rasputin had the power to make things happen. At Villa Rhode, he rarely paid for dinner himself.

As Rasputin's power grew, he spoke out more and more. Many people thought Europe was headed for war. Russia was ready to fight. But Rasputin insisted that going to war would be a mistake. "Fear war!" he told a reporter.

In June 1914, Rasputin went home. Too many people were angry with him. The tsar wanted to go to war. Rasputin's advice made him uncomfortable. Once again, people were saying that Rasputin ruled the country. It was time for Rasputin to escape. He had no idea that he was being followed.

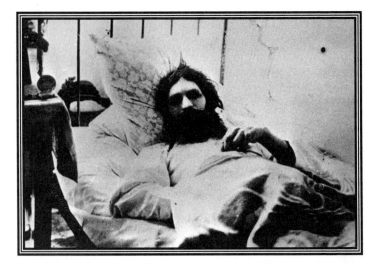

IN 1914, RASPUTIN BARELY ESCAPED DEATH. After he was stabbed in the stomach, he recovered in a hospital in Tyumen.

One afternoon in Siberia, a poor woman came up to Rasputin in the street. Rasputin thought she was a beggar and reached for a coin. The woman pulled a long knife from under her skirt. She plunged it into Rasputin's stomach.

Rasputin staggered off. His attacker ran after him. She tried to stab him again. But a villager grabbed her and pulled her away. Rasputin held his stomach as the blood poured out. He stumbled home, holding his guts in his hands.

The next day, Rasputin was rushed to a hospital in Tyumen. For ten days he was near death. As he lay there, he learned about his attacker. Her name was Khionia Guseva. She was a follower of Iliodor's. And Iliodor had recently disappeared. He had fled across the border into Finland.

By July, Rasputin was feeling better. But Europe was close to war. Without Rasputin, Alexandra was nervous. She sent telegrams to him in Siberia. "We are frightened by the war that threatens us," she said.

"Do you think it might start? Pray for us. Encourage us with your advice."

Rasputin sent messages back. One of them warned Nicholas that "a terrible storm" was coming. "I know that all want war of you," he said. "You are the tsar, the father of your people. Do not let fools triumph. Do not let them do this thing."

Five days later, World War I began.

FROM HIS SICKBED, Rasputin warned the tsar not to go to war.

WORLD WAR I

THE WAR DRAGGED THE WORLD—AND RUSSIA—INTO CHAOS. By 1914, most of Europe was divided among six nations. These nations all wanted power. They built up huge armies and navies. They also looked for allies who would help them in case of war. Germany, Austria-Hungary, and the Ottoman Empire formed the Central Powers. Russia, Great Britain, and France joined together to form the Allies.

In June 1914, a Serbian killed an Austrian prince. In response, Austria-Hungary invaded Serbia. Russia prepared to help defend Serbia. So Germany joined its ally, Austria-Hungary, and declared war on Russia. Then Russia's allies, France and Britain, joined in.

The world was at war. And the world had never seen a war like this. New machine guns, tanks, and poison gas killed soldiers by the thousands.

The war dragged on for four years. Neither Russia, nor Rasputin, would make it to the end.

PART 5

Rasputin and Russia at War

CHAPTER 20

Influence for Sale

RASPUTIN ARRANGES FAVORS—for a fee.

Rasputin returned to the capital late in August. He was still in pain. His stomach was heavily bandaged. But he had survived.

Alexandra was excited to have him back. But she tried to keep their meetings secret. Too many important people hated Rasputin. Alexandra did not want to give his enemies reason to spread rumors.

Rasputin's most important enemy in the fall of 1914 was the tsar's cousin, Grand Duke Nikolai Nikolaevich. The grand duke was once Rasputin's

THE GRAND DUKE NIKOLAI (right) tried to convince the tsar to dismiss Rasputin. The tsar refused to listen.

friend. Now he despised Rasputin. He was furious that the peasant dared to oppose the war.

The grand duke was commander-in-chief of the Russian army. He knew what happened to people who spoke out against Rasputin. But he was bold. He went to Nicholas. He told the tsar that Rasputin was a traitor to Russia. The peasant should go to jail, he said.

Nicholas refused to act. "These are family affairs," he told the grand duke. "They are not a matter for trial." The tsar had spoken. The grand duke turned his attention back to the war.

Safe for now, Rasputin began to use his power. He made a business out of doing favors for people. Rasputin himself was no businessman. A friend named Aron Simanovich took care of that. Simanovich sold jewelry and ran gambling houses. Most of all, though, he was a "fixer." He made friends with important people. Then he used his friendships to get things done. Simanovich often got Grand Duke Nikolai to do favors for him. But Rasputin was his most important friend.

Every day at 10 A.M., people lined up outside Rasputin's apartment. Generals, peasants, and businessmen came to see him. One by one, they came in and asked for favors. Rasputin wrote notes for them. Sometimes, he picked up the telephone and called a government official. Most officials did what he asked out of fear. They did not want Rasputin speaking badly of them to the tsar. Rasputin's enemies didn't keep their jobs for long.

Rasputin could get anything done, it seemed. He

got soldiers released from army duty. That usually cost a few hundred rubles. He got government contracts for Simanovich's business friends. One man wanted to supply the army with coal. For 1,000 rubles, Rasputin set up the deal. Sometimes, Rasputin protected Jews. He helped a group of Jewish dentists get out of jail. The dentists gave him a fur coat to thank him.

Usually, Rasputin took money for his favors. From pretty women, he often asked for something else. One woman was in danger of losing her fortune. She wanted Rasputin to help. "Give me a moment of love and your affair will go along smoothly," Rasputin said. "If there's no love, there's no strength in me and no luck."

Rasputin could have gotten rich as a fixer. But he wasn't interested in the money. He gave some of it away to poor peasants. He spent a lot of it on parties.

The holy man was close to the height of his power. At the same time, both Rasputin and Russia were sinking into chaos.

Drunken Nights

Rasputin begins to spin
OUT OF CONTROL.

EARLY IN HIS LIFE, Rasputin had given up drinking. Once he started again, he couldn't stop.

Police agents now watched Rasputin around the clock. They recorded every drunken party. According to their notes for October 5, 1914, Rasputin was drunk by 6:30 P.M. He passed out in a cab. On October 11, he "came home dead drunk at 1 A.M." He attacked the landlord's wife. The next morning he arrived "dead drunk" again at 7 A.M. He smashed a pane of glass in the door.

It was like this every day. Rasputin did Simanovich's business and received visitors. Women came to see him. His apartment filled with people. Then Rasputin would take them all to a restaurant. He paid for singers. He paid for wine. Finally, in the early morning hours, he went home. The next day, there was a new line. At night, there was a new party.

Rasputin seemed to be destroying himself. He bragged in public about his meetings with the tsar. One night in December, he came home bloody from a fight. In March, he lost control in a Moscow nightclub. He tried to seduce a woman after dinner. She resisted him and he got angry. He smashed mirrors. He pointed to his shirt, which had been made by the tsarina. It was a "gift from the old woman," he bragged. "I do with her what I want." Restaurant staff called the police.

By this time, Grand Duke Nikolai was disgusted with Rasputin. He heard news of Rasputin's drunken outbursts. And he was sick of granting favors. Every week, Simanovich asked the grand duke for his help.

The grand duke told him to stop. He threatened to send Simanovich to Siberia.

Rasputin tried to help. He offered to visit the grand duke at the front. The grand duke wrote back quickly. "If you come I'll have you hanged," he said.

The grand duke tried again with the tsar. He showed the tsar a police report about Rasputin's drunken night in Moscow. The grand duke told Nicholas to show the report to Alexandra. "Put an end to him," the duke said.

But it was not Rasputin who met his end. Alexandra read the report. She refused to believe a word of it. And she was furious with the grand duke. She wrote to the tsar and insisted that he fire his cousin. The grand duke had spoken out against a "Man of God." He had grown too powerful, she told her husband. "Nobody knows who is Emperor now," she said.

Nicholas did not act right away. But in the summer, the Russian army suffered another defeat. Russian soldiers were battling the German army in

Poland. At the time, half of Poland was part of the Russian empire. In July, the Germans took the city of Warsaw. A million Poles were left homeless. They staggered back into Russia with nothing to eat. Many of them died by the side of the road.

The war effort was failing fast. Soldiers died by the thousands. The army had no time to train new soldiers. Many of them had no idea how to use a rifle.

In August, the tsar made his decision. He fired the grand duke. With Alexandra urging him on, the tsar himself became commander-in-chief.

The world was shocked. Nicholas had no training as an army leader. Yet he was taking over an army of six million men.

To command the army, the tsar had to live at the front. Alexandra was left alone in St. Petersburg. With her husband gone, she had decisions to make. She ruled Russia. At her side was her "Friend," the drunken Rasputin.

CHAPTER 22

War at Home

RASPUTIN AND ALEXANDRA take control.

At THE FRONT, Nicholas led the army to bigger and bigger defeats. At home, Alexandra ruled Russia with Rasputin's help. All around them, the country was falling apart.

Many Russians hated the war. Every month, nearly 60,000 men died in battle. The country was spending a fortune on the army. Food was expensive. Prices nearly doubled in the first year of the war. Workers and peasants ate porridge and bread. Eggs, meat, and sugar were hard to find.

RUSSIAN TROOPS BADLY NEEDED WEAPONS
AND FOOD. Here, the tsar brings them
a blessing and a holy icon.

Alexandra stayed in the palace. She met with the ministers, Russia's top government officials. She sent telegrams to the front addressed to "Nicky." Her notes urged the tsar to make decisions. She told him who to fire and who to hire. She told him how to deal with his enemies. Usually, the notes mentioned Rasputin.

The tsar wrote back to Alexandra. He called her "Lovey," or "Wifey." Usually, he took her advice.

A week after the tsar left for the front, Alexandra went after the interior minister. The minister was in charge of the secret police. He had ordered the investigation into Rasputin's outburst in Moscow. Alexandra told Nicholas he should be replaced. The tsar should find someone who would "listen to our Friend's advice," she wrote. In a month, it was done.

Every week, it seemed, Alexandra or Rasputin suggested that someone be replaced. According to Simanovich, the tsar sometimes called Rasputin for advice. Rasputin would put the phone down for a minute. "We need a minister," he would say. Simanovich and others would make suggestions. Rasputin would pass them on to the tsar.

Many of the candidates got important jobs. Some of them paid Rasputin for the favor. Others simply promised to use their new positions to help Rasputin's friends. At one point, Nicholas complained that there were too many changes. "Our Friend's opinions of people are sometimes very strange," he told his wife. "All these changes make my head go round."

Still, the tsar made them anyway. In one year alone, Russia had five interior ministers, three war ministers, four agriculture ministers, and three justice ministers. Many of them were suggested by Rasputin.

Rasputin also influenced the war effort. He told Alexandra that he had visions about the war. She often passed the information on to the tsar. Late in 1915, Rasputin wanted the army to advance near Riga, the capital of Latvia. "He . . . says we can and we must," Alexandra wrote. Other times, she asked the war minister for war plans. She wanted to know when the army was scheduled to attack. That way Rasputin could pray for success.

Success, however, was nowhere in sight. The war was driving Russia to ruin. Rasputin and Alexandra were helping it along.

CHAPTER 23

Dark Forces

A few Russians decide that RASPUTIN MUST GO.

BY 1916, RUSSIANS WERE FED UP with their leaders. Workers went on strike. Peasants stole horses from wealthy landowners. Soldiers deserted the army. In St. Petersburg, workers marched in the streets. "Down with the war!" they shouted. "Give us bread!" Troops were asked to put down the protests. They fired on the police instead.

St. Petersburg was about to explode. Many people blamed the unrest on German agents. And rumor had it that Alexandra and Rasputin were spying for the

Germans. Alexandra, after all, was a German princess. Russians called her the "German woman." She hid a radio in the palace, it was said. At night, she passed secrets to her family in Germany.

The newspapers were full of scandal. And Rasputin was at the center of it all. Some people said he was involved with Alexandra. Supposedly, his underwear flew over the palace instead of the Russian flag. In the spring, the interior minister accused Rasputin of spying for the Germans.

The tsar was in danger once again. He had lost control of the country. Troops were refusing to fight. The tsarina ruled the nation. And Rasputin was said to control her. Many of the tsar's supporters felt that Rasputin had to go. The head of the secret police offered him 200,000 rubles to get out of town.

Rasputin fought back. He insisted that he was saving Russia from destruction. "The fools don't understand who I am," he told a reporter. "If they burn me, Russia is finished. They'll bury us together."

On November 19, 1916, a politician named Vladimir Purishkevich decided to speak out. He stood up in the Duma. Purishkevich desperately wanted to save the monarchy. He was convinced that Rasputin was destroying it. He called Rasputin a "filthy . . . corrupt peasant." It was time to stop the "dark forces" that controlled Russia, he said.

Purishkevich's speech was read all over St. Petersburg. One man was particularly impressed. Prince Felix Yusupov had heard the speech in the Duma. Two days later, he went to visit Purishkevich. The time for speeches was over, Yusupov said. Rasputin must be killed. Purishkevich agreed. Together, he and Yusupov began to plan Rasputin's murder.

CHAPTER 24

Iced

RASPUTIN WAS GONE, but
Russia's problems weren't over.

RASPUTIN'S DEATH was as strange as his life.
On December 29, Rasputin went for tea at Yusupov's
palace. He survived Yusupov's poisoned cakes and
wine. But he never got a chance to meet Irina.

Yusupov eventually told the story of the
murder to police. He claimed that he shot Rasputin
while the holy man prayed. Then Yusupov called
his friends downstairs. They decided that Rasputin
was dead. The friends left to get ready for the next
part of the plan.

In a half-hour, Yusupov went back alone. He leaned down to take Rasputin's pulse. Rasputin jumped up and grabbed him by the shoulder. Still bleeding, he tried to strangle Yusupov. The prince freed himself and ran upstairs in horror.

The men ran outside to see Rasputin running away. Purishkevich took out his pistol. He aimed carefully and shot Rasputin twice.

The murderers then wrestled the body into the trunk of a car. They drove through the darkened streets to the Petrovsky Bridge. At dawn, they threw Rasputin's body into the freezing water of the Neva River.

Later, an autopsy revealed that there was water in Rasputin's lungs. He had still been breathing when he was thrown into the Neva.

Days later, Rasputin was buried near the tsar's palace. Nicholas and Alexandra went to the funeral.

Nobles all across Russia celebrated Rasputin's death. Some wrote to Yusupov to thank him. But Rasputin had predicted that these nobles wouldn't last long after his death. He was soon proved right.

In January 1918, 300,000 workers went on strike in St. Petersburg. By February, soldiers were joining them in the streets. Troops broke into jails and freed prisoners. They raided the mansions where Rasputin had been a guest.

The tsar rushed home from the front, but his train was delayed by the protests. Alexandra prayed at Rasputin's grave for strength. She wrote to her husband. She told him to wear the cross that Rasputin gave him.

Protesters demanded that the tsar give up his throne. On March 15, Nicholas II stepped down. He was the last tsar to rule Russia.

In October, Communists took power. They found the tsar's family under guard in Siberia. The family was taken to Ekaterinburg, 300 miles from Rasputin's village. They were executed in the summer of 1918.

Alexandra and her daughters wore lockets around their necks when they were buried. Inside the lockets were pictures of Rasputin.

~~~~~~~~~~~~~~~

Wicked?

~~~~~~~~~~~~~~~

RASPUTIN DIED IN 1916. But his legend lived on. People all over the world wanted gossip about Rasputin and the royal family. And many of those who had known Rasputin were eager to provide it. Rasputin's murderers, Purishkevich and Yusupov, wrote about him. So did his friends, Sasonov and Simanovich. Maria Rasputin wrote two books about her father. Movies came out in 1917, 1932, and 1966. Even the police chief in charge of spying on Rasputin wrote about him.

These days, Rasputin's name stands for a kind of evil. A "rasputin" is someone who cares only about power. He is clever and sneaky. He controls people from behind the scenes.

But was Rasputin really evil? He certainly wanted power. He was a poor peasant boy who came to the big city. He loved to brag about his influence over the tsar.

Sometimes Rasputin used his influence to help people. Often he used it to put corrupt people in positions of power. Those people made decisions that may have sent soldiers to their deaths during World War I. Still, Rasputin never killed anyone himself. In fact, he tried to keep Russia out of this terrible war.

And what about Rasputin's religious faith? He said he was a holy man. Many people believed him. Some of them claimed that Rasputin saved their lives. Yet this "holy man" drank wildly. He used his reputation to seduce women.

Rasputin was a complicated man. During his lifetime, people either loved him or hated him. They rarely understood him. Was he sincerely religious? Or did he use his faith to gain power—over women and the royal family? Did he use people for his own gain? Or did they use him? Did Rasputin destroy Russia? Or did Russia destroy Rasputin?

What do you think: Was Rasputin truly wicked?

Timeline of Terror

1869

January 22, 1869: Rasputin is born in Pokrovskoye, a town in Siberia.

Summer 1878: Dimitri, Rasputin's brother, dies.

1883: Rasputin has a vision and thinks he sees God.

1888: Rasputin and Praskovya marry. Soon after, Rasputin visits a monastery at Verkhoturye. He spends the next few years as a wandering holy man.

1897-1900: Rasputin's three children—Dimitri, Varvara, and Maria—are born.

1903: Rasputin arrives in St. Petersburg and meets important religious leaders.

1904: Alexis, heir to the throne, is born with hemophilia. Russia and Japan go to war.

1905: Rasputin is introduced to the tsar and tsarina. Russian workers and peasants riot against the tsar.

1907: Rasputin convinces Tsarina Alexandra that he can heal her son. He becomes a frequent guest.

1910: Rumors surface about Rasputin's "unholy" dealings with women.

1911: Bishop Hermogen and Iliodor accuse Rasputin in public.

1914: Rasputin survives assassination attempt. World War I begins.

August 1915: Tsar takes command of troops, leaving Alexandra and Rasputin to run the country.

December 29, 1916: Rasputin goes for tea with Prince Yusupov.

1916

GLOSSARY

barge (BARJ) *noun* a long boat with a flat bottom

bishop (BISH-uhp) *noun* a senior priest in the Russian Orthodox Church

chaos (KAY-oss) *noun* total confusion

corrupt (kuh-RUHPT) *adjective* dishonest in business dealings

cult (KUHLT) *noun* a group of people strongly devoted to a religion, idea, or way of life

drought (DROUT) *noun* a long period of very dry weather

duma (DOO-ma) *noun* a representative assembly that Tsar Nicholas II set up in response to the Revolution of 1905

elder (EL-duhr) *noun* a respected holy man who lives a simple life

fast (FAST) *verb* to give up eating food for a time

heir (AIR) *noun* the person next in line to the throne

hemophilia (hee-muh-FIL-ee-uh) *noun* a disease that prevents a person's blood from clotting properly

hereditary (huh-RED-uh-ter-ee) *adjective* passed from parent to child

icon (EYE-kon) *noun* a picture of a holy figure

incense (IN-senss) *noun* a substance that is burned to give off a sweet smell; sometimes used in religious ceremonies

khlysty (KLY-stee) *noun* a cult that urged people to sin to get closer to God

manifesto (man-ih-FEST-oh) *noun* a written statement of a person's or peoples' views

monarchy (MON-ark-ee) *noun* a country led by a ruler who inherits his or her position

monastery (MON-uh-ster-ee) *noun* a group of buildings where monks live and work

123

monk (MUHNGK) *noun* a man who lives in a religious community and has promised to devote his life to God

muzhik (moo-ZHEEK) *noun* a Russian peasant

penance (PEN-uhnss) *noun* an act one performs to show that one is sorry for a sin

pilgrimage (PIL-gruhm-ij) *noun* a journey to a holy place

pneumonia (noo-MOH-nyuh) *noun* a serious disease that causes the lungs to become filled with thick fluid, making breathing difficult

pogroms (POH-grumz) *noun* anti-Jewish riots in Russia in the early 1900s

porridge (POR-ij) *noun* a food made by boiling grains in milk or water until the mixture is thick

repent (ri-PENT) *verb* to feel sorry for one's sins and try to make up for them

revolution (rev-uh-LOO-shuhn) *noun* an uprising by the people of a country that changes the country's system of government

ruble (ROO-buhl) *noun* the main unit of money in Russia

Russian Orthodox Church (RUHSH-in OR-thuh-doks CHURCH) *noun* the main Christian church of Russia

shtetls (SHTET-ilz) *noun* small, poor, Jewish villages in Russia

sin (SIN) *noun* bad or evil behavior

tsar (ZAR) *noun* the emperor of Russia before the Russian Revolution of 1917

tsarevich (ZAR-eh-vitch) *noun* the heir to the throne in Russia

tsarina (zar-EE-nuh) *noun* the wife of a tsar

vision (VIZH-uhn) *noun* something seen in a dream or trance that is viewed as a sign from God

vodka (VOD-ka) *noun* a type of liquor popular in Russia

FIND OUT MORE

Here are some books and Web sites with more information about Rasputin and his times.

BOOKS

Britton, Beverly. **Hemophilia**. San Diego, CA: Lucent Books, 2003. (112 pages)
For more about the disease hemophilia and why it occurs.

Hatt, Christine. **World War I, 1914-1918 (Documenting History)**. New York: Franklin Watts, 2001. (62 pages) *The story of World War I told through primary source documents.*

Kent, Zachary. **World War I: The War to End Wars (American War Series)**. Hillside NJ: Enslow Publishers, 2000. (128 pages) *The complete story of World War I.*

Massie, Robert K. **Nicholas and Alexandra**. New York: Ballantine Books, 2000. (613 pages) *A great book about this time period for the ambitious reader.*

Rogers, Stillman D. **Russia (Enchantment of the World)**. New York: Children's Press, 2002. (144 pages) *Information about the history, people, and geography of Russia.*

Ross, Stewart. **The Russian Revolution (Events and Outcomes)**. Austin TX: Raintree Steck-Vaughn, 2003. (78 pages) *For the full story of the Russian revolutions of 1905 and 1917.*

WEB SITES

http://news.bbc.co.uk/2/hi/special_report/1998/10/98/world_war_i/197437.stm
The BBC created this site to mark the 80th anniversary of World War I.

http://www.loc.gov/rr/frd/ *The Library of Congress has a great collection of country studies. Go to this site, select "country studies," then choose Russia from the list of countries.*

http://www.mayoclinic.com/health/hemophilia/DS00218 *A medical explanation of hemophilia from the Mayo Clinic.*

http://www.nicholasandalexandra.com/ *This website was created for an exhibit that toured the U.S. in 1999–2001.*

http://www.pbs.org/weta/faceofrussia/intro.html *PBS created this site, called "The Face of Russia."*

For Grolier subscribers:

http://go.grolier.com/ **searches:** Nicholas II; Alexandra Fyodorovna; Rasputin; Alexis Petrovich; Anastasia; hemophilia; World War I; Russian Revolution

INDEX

127

Authors' Note and Bibliography

Rasputin was a man of many contradictions. Stories were bound to grow up around him. Many of those stories came in part from the imagination of his own daughter, Maria. Others were spread by his enemies. Some were written down by people who were in a position to know the truth. It has been our task to determine truth from fiction about Rasputin.

As you read this book keep several questions in mind. Do you consider Rasputin to have been wicked? If so, why? If not, how do you explain the hatred towards him? Or were Nicholas and Alexandra ultimately responsible for the murder of Rasputin by not revealing the illness of their son?

The following books have been most useful in telling Rasputin's story.

Dobson, Christopher. **Prince Felix Yusupov: The Man Who Murdered Rasputin.** London: Harrap, 1989.

Fuhrmann, Joseph, T. **Rasputin: A Life.** New York: Praeger, 1990.

Massie, Robert K. **Nicholas and Alexandra.** New York: Atheneum, 1967.

Monahan, Brian. **The Saint Who Sinned.** London: Aurum Press, 1998.

Potts, D. M. and Potts, W. T. W. **Queen Victoria's Gene.** Gloucestershire, UK: Sutton, 1999.

Radzinsky, Edward. **The Rasputin File.** New York: Doubleday, 2000.

Rasputin, Maria and Barham, Patte. **Rasputin: The Man Behind the Myth.** Englewood Cliffs, NJ: Prentice Hall Inc., 1977.

We are grateful to Jackie Carter, Shari Joffe, and Elizabeth Ward for their work on this project.

Special thanks to our editor, Tod Olson.

—Enid A. Goldberg and Norman Itzkowitz